The Tomb of Queen Nefertari

Egyptian Gods and Goddesses
of the New Kingdom

Books and Cards by Ruth Shilling

ruthshilling.com

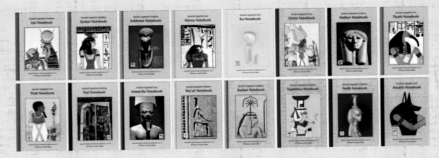

Pictures of Ancient Egyptian Gods & Goddesses: Edited Photos

Egyptian Gods & Goddesses Notebooks: Blank Papyrus-Imprint Pages, Vol. 1-16

Time & Space in the Temples & Pyramids: All One World Egypt Tour

SINAI: The Desert & Bedouins of South Sinai's Central Regions (photos & text)

Accessing Clear Guidance: Help and Answers Through Inspired Writing & Inner Knowing

Clear & Free of Unwanted Thoughts & Emotions: 25 Effective Methods

Violin Success Series
• Success with the Violin & Life: Strategies, Techniques, and Tips for Learning Quickly and Doing Well, Volume 1
• Performing at Your Best: A Musician's Guide to Successful Performances, Volume 2

Through A Medium's Eyes Series: About Life, Love, Mediumship, and the Spirit World
• Rev. B. Anne Gehman, Volume 1 (also in LARGE PRINT)
• Carol Gasber, Volume 2
• Neal Rzepkowski, M.D., Volume 3

The Color It True Manifestation Mandala Series, Volumes 1-4

Ancient Egyptian Gods & Goddess Cards: godsgoddessescards.com

The Tomb of
Queen Nefertari

Egyptian Gods and Goddesses
of the New Kingdom

RUTH SHILLING

All One World Books & Media

The Tomb of Queen Nefertari:
Egyptian Gods & Goddesses of the New Kingdom

Print book ISBN: 978-1-945963-22-3

eBook ISBN: 978-1-945963-23-0

Published by All One World Books & Media

all1world.com

Text, interior illustrations, photo edits, and cover design: Ruth Shilling

The photos of the Nefertari tomb were taken by Ruth Shilling and All One World Egypt Tours participants. They have given permission to use their photos. Special thanks to Ruth Stockey and Barbara Madar. Note that the photos have been edited and some do not show all the imperfections found on the original walls.

Ruth Shilling: ruthshilling.com
Ancient Egyptian Gods & Goddess Cards: godsgoddessescards.com

FACEBOOK PAGES
Egyptian Gods and Goddesses: facebook.com/EgyptGodsGoddesses
Ruth Shilling: facebook.com/ruthshillingmm
Egypt Tours: facebook.com/1worldtours

*Above: What one sees first from
the doorway of the tomb*

*Previous page: Queen Nefertari
QV 66, Tomb of Nefertari, Luxor, Egypt*

Table of Contents

- 1 -
Nefertari's Name

Nefertari

"The Beautiful Companion"

It is easy for people to confuse Queen Nefertari with Queen Nefertiti because their names both start with the same Ancient Egyptian word, *nefer.*

Nefer = Beautiful and Good

Queen Nefertari was the wife of Ramesses II ("Ramesses the Great"). Her name is translated, "The Beautiful Companion."

Queen Nefertiti was the wife of Akhenaten. Her name is translated, "The Beautiful One Has Come."

There isn't agreement among Egyptologists about what the *nefer* hieroglyph actually represents. It looks like a lute, a musical instrument that is similar to a guitar. If you were sitting outside on a summer evening and heard in the distance someone plucking gently on a guitar, you might say, "That sounds lovely – beautiful and good." Whether that is what the hieroglyph is truly picturing or not, that is a good way to remember and recognize it.

Royal Names

The royal names in Ancient Egypt were shown in a **cartouche**. This is an elongated circle with a line at the bottom. It is thought that this shape was originally a label. A name could be written on the long, flat part and the bar at the bottom held a string that could then be tied around jars or other items that needed to be labeled.

When Napoleon's army arrived in Egypt in 1798, the French soldiers saw this shape on the walls of the monuments and started calling them cartouches because the shape was similar to their powder cartridges (ammunition). That French word is still used today for the shape surrounding the Ancient Egyptian royal names.

Eternity

The Ancient Egyptian *shen* hieroglyph means *eternity* or *infinity*. It is a circle with a bar at the bottom. When that circle is stretched out, it forms the cartouche shape. Putting a name within the *eternity sign* brings eternal life to the person with that name.

Hieroglyph = Sacred Symbol

There were three forms of writing used in Ancient Egypt – hieroglyphic, hieratic, and demotic. The word *hieroglyph* is a combination of the word *hiero* (sacred, holy) and *glyph* (symbol, sign). The holy writing, hieroglyphic, was used in the temples and tombs. *Hieratic* was similar to a shorthand the scribes used for writing sacred texts on papyri. *Demotic* writing was used for business and other secular transactions.

The **Rosetta Stone** has a text written in three languages – hieroglyphic, demotic, and Greek. It was the cartouches which gave the clue to the meaning of the hieroglyphs. Once it was clear that anything in that shape was the name of a king, the symbols could be matched up with the royal names that were already known in Greek. The hieroglyphs were first deciphered in 1822.

The writing on the walls of Nefertari's tomb was for a sacred purpose (helping her in the afterlife), so it is written in hieroglyphic.

The individual hieroglyphic signs (hieroglyphs) can be used in three different ways – to communicate a whole concept, as an alphabetical letter, or to represent a group of letters.

Reading Nefertari's Cartouche

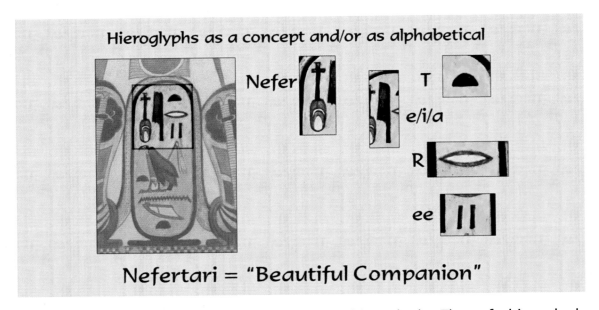

Hieroglyphs as a concept and/or as alphabetical

Nefer

T

e/i/a

R

ee

Nefertari = "Beautiful Companion"

Above is Nefertari's cartouche with her name in hieroglyphs. The *nefer* hieroglyph (the one that looks like a lute) is "beautiful and good" (or simply "beautiful") and is the beginning of her name.

The half circle is the **letter T** and represents a loaf of bread. Adding it to a word can make that word feminine in the same way that the modern names Paul becomes Paulette, or George becomes Georgette. However, the T-glyph does not always make words feminine. Often it is simply alphabetical, a letter in a word.

lord

lady

son

daughter of Ra

Examples of the T-glyph changing a word from masculine to feminine are the way *lord/lady* and *son/daughter* are written. The dish shape is *neb* and means "lord of" when placed above another word (when it is below, it means "all," as in "all the gods"). The goose is the hieroglyph for "the child of" and the exclusion/inclusion of the T-glyph makes it clear if it is a son or daughter. In this example, the red circle is the God Ra (also written *Re*), so it is saying, "daughter of Ra."

In Nefertari's name, the **HALF-CIRCLE** is the letter T, the beginning of "tari."

The **FEATHER** is similar to a vowel sound. The vowels were not written in this language, but the feather represents a sound that is similar to an *e, i,* or *a*.

The **LETTER R** is a mouth. Looking at it, it's easy to think of the "R-r-r-r-r" sound the mouth would be making. Each glyph is also a particular color. You can see here that the mouth has red lips and white teeth inside of the lips. The Ra hieroglyph on the previous page in the "daughter of Ra" is red because Ra is the sun. The color yellow can sometimes be substituted for the color red, but in Nefertari's tomb, the circle symbolizing Ra is consistently painted red.

The **TWO STROKES** at the bottom that look like the number 11 are an abbreviation for two of the feathers. A sense of balance, harmony, and beauty was of the utmost importance to the Ancient Egyptians. If there were two more feathers in her cartouche, it would have given it a less pleasing visual effect. The two vertical lines were an acceptable substitute, so could be used at the artist's discretion. The two strokes are also the way the number two is written in hieroglyphs.

The bottom part of Nefertari's cartouche tells us which goddess Nefertari is most aligned with – the mother-goddess, Mut, represented as a vulture.

In a sense, one could think of the Goddess Mut as her guardian angel, accompanying her throughout her life. The vulture is also the sign for "mother." If the vulture has the flail (the upside-down V shape tucked under her wing) she is not simply "mother" but the Goddess Mut.

People often ask how it is that the Ancient Egyptians chose the vulture to symbolize motherhood. Of course, it is not possible for us to know that for sure, but in general, the animals that were chosen to represent the different gods and goddesses of Ancient Egypt had qualities in everyday life that mirrored qualities of the gods and goddesses.

For example, in the natural world, vultures are not killers. Unlike the birds of prey – like hawks – the vulture takes that which has already died and feeds it to her children. As it nourishes her young ones, the animal that perished is given new life. It is also said that the vulture will stand in the hot sun with her wings outstretched for hours just to create some shade for her little ones, thus sacrificing her own comfort for her children.

So, the vulture symbolizes the nurturing, self-sacrificing mother. You could think of her as resembling a Mediterranean grandmother from Italy or Greece. She is hunched over, has a wizened face, and wears black. She is constantly focused on the welfare of her family and gives all she can to her children.

Goddess Mut
(vulture)

Beloved of

"Beloved of the Goddess Mut"

In Nefertari's cartouche, underneath the vulture Goddess Mut, there is a zigzag line. This zigzag is used in a number of ways. It can be the letter N, the symbol for water, or used as a preposition. In this case, it is the **preposition OF**.

Underneath the zigzag line is a sideways V followed by the half-circle T. The sideways V is the word for **love or beloved**, and the half-circle makes it feminine.

You may have noticed that there are two snakes on either side of this cartouche. The rearing cobra was a generic symbol for "goddess." It could be used in the names of deities to designate them as a goddess, but it was also a particular goddess. It's the same way a person might call a facial tissue a "Kleenex" even when it is a different brand.

In this case, the goddess on the left wearing the red crown is named Wadjet, the protective goddess of Lower Egypt (the Nile Delta region). The one on the right is named Nekhbet, the protective goddess of Upper Egypt (the higher land up the Nile River). There is more about these two goddesses in Chapter 11.

Nefertari, Beloved (Meri) of Mut

If you look closely at these two Nefertari cartouches,
you will notice some differences.

Two ways to write
"Meri" (love, beloved)

hoe
for loosening soil
(farming)

channel
water canal or
spinning wheel groove

The Ancient Egyptian word for love or beloved was **meri**. It is sounds like the modern name Mary. There were many Ancient Egyptian women who had the word *meri* as part of their name.

At the bottom of Nefertari's cartouche, the hieroglyph for love or beloved is different. There were actually two hieroglyphic signs that mean *meri* (love, beloved). The one on the left is a farming tool similar to the modern grub hoe. The one on the right is understood to be a water channel, but could also be something like the groove in a spinning wheel (seen from above). Either way, it represented something moving between two walls or sides.

These two signs were used interchangeably, so both were correct. It appears to be an artistic decision as to which one was used.

You may have also noticed that the Goddess Mut is at the top in the cartouche on the right but in the middle on the left. When writing a person's name, the gods and goddesses are usually placed at the top (or beginning if it is sideways) because deities are superior and have a higher "rank" than people. We see here that although there were definite artistic codes, there was also flexibility with how the writing was presented.

At right: Queen Nefertari playing the senet game

- 11 -

Nefertari's
Place in History

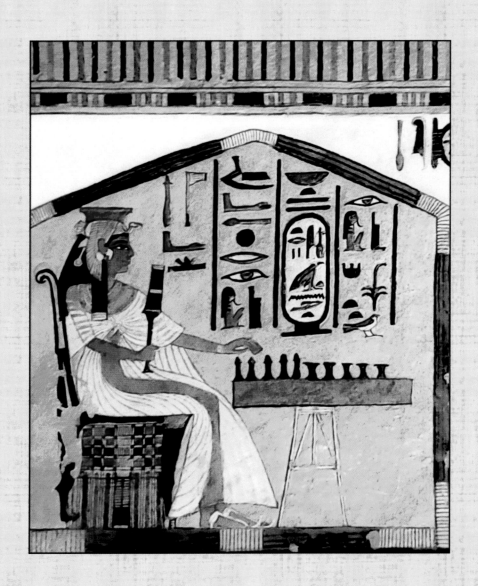

A Brief Look at Ancient Egyptian History

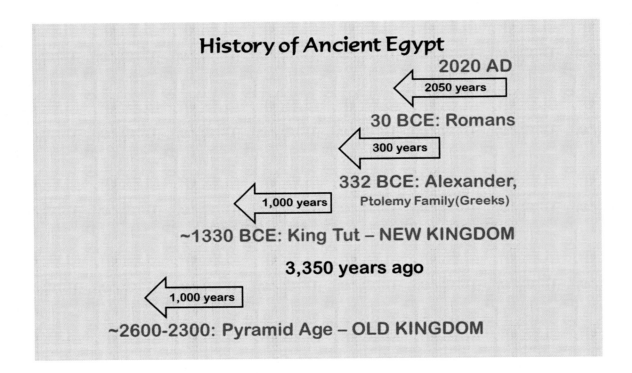

When people watch shows on TV about Egypt, they can get the feeling that "Ancient Egypt" was pretty much the same over 3,000 years of history. This is not true. An example of this is the Exodus movie where Moses is with Ramesses II (Nefertari's husband) and slaves are building the pyramids. Ramesses II was in the New Kingdom. The pyramids had already existed for at least 1,000 years. Another misleading idea is that the country was ruled in a stable, continuous way for 3,000 years. Again, this is not true. What is well documented is that there were a series of rises and falls, stability and chaos, prosperity and famine.

During these different periods, the centers of government changed locations, the writing was altered, there were shifts in which gods and goddesses were prominent, the style of art changed, and the myths and stories changed as well. There were times that invaders overtook the country from different directions. The invaders that came into Egypt before the New Kingdom brought horses and chariots to Egypt for the first time.

It was not until the Arab conquest during 639 – 646 AD (not BCE) that camels were introduced. The wheels that turned Egypt were always the donkeys!

On the most basic level, someone new to the history of Ancient Egypt can best begin to get a feeling for the magnitude of it by learning three major time periods: the **Old Kingdom** or pyramid age, the **New Kingdom** (Nefertiti, King Tut, Nefertari...) and the Ptolemaic or **Greek period**. The Greeks ruled Egypt for about 300 years. They lived in Egypt but kept themselves separate from the Egyptian population. The first Greek ruler of Egypt to learn the Egyptian language was Cleopatra VII, the one known today as the famous Queen Cleopatra. So, although she lived in Egypt and ruled the country, she was not an Egyptian. She was Greek. When Cleopatra died in 30 BCE, the Romans took over.

Going back 1,000 years before the time that Alexander the Great entered Egypt in 332 BCE (beginning of the Greek rulers), we find ourselves at the time of King Tutankhamen ("King Tut"), right in the middle of what is called the New Kingdom. Exact dates vary, depending on which source you are using, but the New Kingdom dates are approximately 1550 – 1077 BCE.

NEW KINGDOM
1550 – 1077 BCE

1479-1425 BCE: Hatshepsut, Thutmosis III

1391-1353 BCE: Amenhotep III

1353-1336 BCE: Akhenaten & Nefertiti

1334-1324 BCE: King Tut – middle of NEW KINGDOM

1290-1279 BCE: Seti 1

Ramesses II "The Great" (~ 1303-1213 BCE)
Reigned 1279-1213
Queen Nefertari (~ 1301-1255 BCE)
"Great Royal Wife"

What is a Pharaoh?

King

When someone says the word *pharaoh* today, it is understood that they are referring to an Ancient Egyptian king. However, in the same way that the news media in the USA reports that "the White House issued the following statement..." the word *pharaoh* actually means "Great House," i.e., "the government." The Ancient Egyptian word is *per-aa*, and that became the modern word, *pharaoh*. The Ancient Egyptian word for king is *Nesu*. To the left is the hieroglyph for *king*. On page 19 you will see how it fits into a hieroglyphic inscription.

What is a Great Royal Wife?

Nefertari married Ramesses II before he was crowned king. When he became king, she held the title of "Great Royal Wife." In the same way that "Vice-President" is a governmental position, the role of Great Royal Wife was also a particular role. Part of being a Great Royal Wife was to be the kings companion for public appearances. Nefertari's first born child was a boy who became heir to the throne. However, he died while Ramesses II was still ruling.

Ramesses II and Nefertari were close in age. She was probably about two years younger. While Nefertari probably died in her early 40's, Ramesses lived to the age of 90 and ruled for 67 years. During that time, he sired more than 100 children with many different wives, 4-5 of whom held the position of Great Royal Wife.

There was another queen, Isetnofret (also spelled *Isenofre*), who held the position of Great Royal Wife during the same time that Queen Nefertari did. After they both died, their daughters, Merytamen and Bint-Anath, both held the "Great Royal Wife" title. Tour guides in Egypt like to say that Queen Nefertari was Ramesses II's favorite wife. This may or may not be true. His name for her was "For Whom the Sun Rises and Sets," which sounds good, but what he actually felt in his heart no one can say for sure.

The Nefertari Temple at Abu Simbel

The Abu Simbel site is said to be where the goddesses dwelled who created the annual Nile flooding. There were two caves there which were sacred to these goddesses. Ramesses II turned those caves into two temples. The larger one was dedicated to four masculine gods, one of whom was himself! The other three gods were Ptah, Amun, and Ra-Horakhty.

The smaller temple was for the Goddess Hathor and was dedicated to Queen Nefertari. Dedicating a temple to a queen was very out of the ordinary, but since Ramesses had included himself as a god in the other temple, it may have seemed like it followed to dedicate the second temple to his queen, Nefertari. However, he did not represent her as a deity, the way he did himself in the larger temple.

Something else that may have influenced his decision was that he was replacing the sacred place of the Nile-flood-producing goddesses (the story of *which* goddesses varied) with a temple to masculine gods, including himself. Such an action could have angered the goddesses. So keeping one of the temples to honor a feminine deity (Hathor) was probably a wise move. The feminine forces that nurture the nation through life-giving waters were not to be pushed aside!

The historical records of the time show that Queen Nefertari had already died by the time the Nefertari temple was opened. One of her daughters was the feminine counterpart to the king during the opening ceremony.

- III -

Reading the Walls

The Walls Speak

Many of the names used today for the Ancient Egyptian gods and goddesses are the Greek versions of their names. Below is a list of some of the name changes.

Wsir → Osiris   Aset (or Iset) → Isis   Nebhwt → Nephthys

Heru → Horus   Hwt-her→ Hathor   Serket → Selket

Djeuti → Thoth   Inpu → Anubis

Recognizing the names of a few of the gods and goddesses can greatly enhance your enjoyment of Queen Nefertari's tomb. The first two to start with are the God Osiris and his consort/wife, Isis.

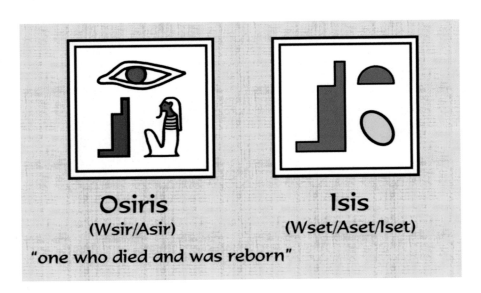

Osiris
(Wsir/Asir)

Isis
(Wset/Aset/Iset)

"one who died and was reborn"

The name of Osiris is used repeatedly in the New Kingdom tombs because it is often being used as an adjective. There is a story about Osiris being killed and then being brought back to life. So, the name of Osiris is used to say, "the one who died and was reborn." If the walls say that Nefertari is the Osiris queen, that means that she has been reborn into the afterlife. She continues to live.

Page 14: Horus, Son of Isis. Page 15: "Sema-Tawy" –
Unity of the Two Lands, Upper & Lower Egypt   *At right: Young Horus as a priest*

Words spoken by...

Another helpful set of hieroglyphs to recognize are the ones that mean, "Words spoken by..." If you see someone on the wall that looks like a god or goddess, or maybe a king or queen, looking for this group of signs will signal that their name is either directly underneath, or is written shortly thereafter.

Putting together some of what has already been covered in this book, you may be able to read some of the wall below.

Words spoken by

Horus **(hawk)**
(Heru)

Son of **(goose)**

Up to right:
Isis
(throne, bread, egg)

The goose was explained on page 4.

The name of the goddess Isis is on page 16.

You may also recognize the KING hieroglyph near the top right of this picture. See that glyph on page 12.

Here is another wall to read. The full picture is on page v.

Words spoken by

Osiris
(one who is reborn)
eye, throne, seated deity

Queen
(wife of the king)
plant, basket, bread

the great
bird, mouth, bread

Words spoken by the great reborn (Osiris) queen, Nefertari Beloved of Mut

Reading Symbols

In the year 2000, a friend sent me an email which she ended with this:

:)

I had no idea why she was putting a colon and part of a parentheses into the email. When I asked her why she did that, she said it was a smile. "That doesn't look like a smile," I said. She needed to explain to me that it was sideways. Of course, now when I see it, I can't *not* see it as a smile. This is the way it is with communications in symbolic form. If you do not know what they mean, you just miss the communication all together. If you do know, the meaning is obvious.

If you live in the United States and you see a cartoon with an elephant and a donkey having an interaction, you interpret it as a political cartoon with some sort of message about the Republican and Democratic parties. If you did not know the symbolism of those two animals in that context, you might see that the artist had done a nice job drawing the elephant. You would be able to appreciate it on that level, but you would miss the communication of the cartoon.

Likewise, people who look at Ancient Egyptian art may look at it and appreciate the beauty and balance of the images, but not have the knowledge that this is a set of symbols that are *communicating*. The artworks that have been painted or carved into the walls of the tombs and temples are actually stories in themselves. Like the modern-day cartoons, when we learn their symbolic language, we have a much richer experience of them.

Ancient Egyptian Art is a Symbolic Language, (not a copy of what we see)

When people today look at the walls in Egypt, it is not surprising that they expect the images there to look like the pictures they are accustomed to seeing. Especially now that we all take photos, it's easy to think that the artwork should convert what we see in 3D to a two-dimensional surface in the same way, that it should look like what our eyes see.

Paintings in our museums and photography online capture vibrant sunsets, beautiful faces, flowers, nature... The artwork gives us a window into the artist's perspectives on life and looking at their art can enhance our own way of seeing the world. So when we look at the walls of an Ancient Egyptian tomb it makes sense that we don't realize that **these beautiful images are not trying to look like a photograph.**

The images on the walls are a pictorial code, a living language in symbols.

Page 21: Horus, Son of Isis, and Queen Nefertari

Each scene in Queen Nefertari's tomb is **a group of symbols in the forms that they will be most easily and quickly recognized.**

For example, how easy is it to read these symbols? Turn the page, then turn the whole book upside down and find a different set of images there. Which could you read most quickly?

A **FOOT** is easiest to recognize when we see it sideways, so in Ancient Egyptian art, it is shown that way. Note that the arch of the foot is shown here on both feet, so they are technically both right feet. Showing left and right feet differently is not needed. We only need to know that there are two legs with two feet.

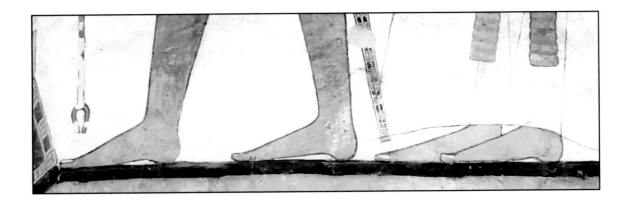

There is artwork from the New Kingdom period where the artist has chosen to have a right and left foot, but that is not common. In this case, drawing the feet with the arch could also be a way to give them more buoyancy. Horus and Nefertari are not walking in a heavy, flat-footed way.

Another subtle but clear difference is that Horus has one foot forward and Nefertari's are closer together. The statues of Ancient Egypt show men and gods with one foot forward. They are active, masculine; their strength and value is in what they DO. The women and goddesses were shown with feet closer together – their feminine strength is in their stability and constancy, an "always there" reliability. Their strength and value is in what they ARE.

A notable exception to this is the Goddess Sekhmet, the lioness, who embodies the active-feminine force. Her standing statues show her with one foot forward.

Regarding masculine and feminine, it is noteworthy that while the sky is feminine (Nut), the earth (Geb), moon (Thoth, Khonsu), and sun (Ra) are all masculine.

FACES are shown in profile. Law enforcement officials and artists know that a person's profile is the easiest way to clearly identify someone.

EYES are shown looking at them head on, which is again, the easiest way to recognize that shape.

CROWNS. An interesting contrast here (left) is that the crown worn by Horus is seen from the side, but Nefertari's crown is seen looking at it from the front. In both cases that is the easiest way to know what those crowns actually look like. So this shows that the convention is not dictated by the item, but rather, by the ease in recognition.

HANDS and GESTURES

As with the feet, you can see below that Nefertari is not pictured with a right and left hand. Both hands match. Again, we only need to know that there are two arms with two hands. It is, however, important to know which hand gesture is being expressed.

Nefertari, see page v.

Honoring, praising, worshipping. Here, Nefertari has her two hands up in a slightly cupped position. This is the sign for honoring someone, worshipping, or giving praise.

24

Ba Bird. At left, Nefertari is pictured with her *Ba* behind her. The *Ba* is usually understood to be a person's soul or spirit. The symbolism indicates that it is an aspect of ourselves that can think, hear and see (our human head) but has the ability to fly. If the Ancient Egyptians were able to do out-of-body travel, this would be the perfect symbol for that. Although it is not that way in the example above, the Ba is often represented behind the person with two little arms up in the same "honoring" gesture.

BLESSING, comfort. The one-hand-up-slightly-cupped gesture is usually done by the deities, not the humans. If you reach out to someone to give them comfort or a blessing, this is how your hand would probably look. If your hand was up and you were saying, "Stop!" your hand would be tight with fingers arched back, not cupped.

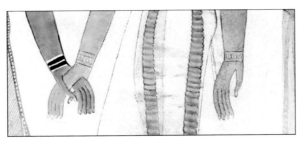

HOLDING HANDS. Here the God Horus is holding Nefertari's hand which shows that they have a good relationship. He accepts and approves of her and is helping her in her afterlife journey.

Men, darker skin. The men in Ancient Egypt were represented having darker skin than the women. This shows they are doing activities outside, while the women are indoors. Horus is a male deity, so he has darker skin than Nefertari. The goddesses are divine (= golden), so they have yellow skin while Nefertari is more flesh-toned.

The upside-down symbols at left are for comparison to the symbols on page 22.

Ma'at   *Selket*

READY TO HUG. The open arms and wings above let us know that the Goddess Ma'at is in the "let's hug" gesture. If you look closely at the way it is drawn, you can see that the arms and hands match (not right/left) and that the right arm begins in the middle of her chest, rather than back at her shoulder. Representing it this way communicates to us that her arms are open *and* that her wings begin in the middle of her back. So the wings are a combination of being shown from the back and from the side. The lovely thing is that all of this information is easily understood by the viewer in an quick and efficient way without even needing to think about it. You may also have noticed above that in front of Ma'at, there is an eternity symbol *(shen)* that is being attached (given) to the cartouche of Nefertari. Read: "The Goddess Ma'at is giving eternal life to Nefertari."

Note that throughout Nefertari's tomb, the deities she encounters are all supporting and helping her – holding her hand, showing their approval and support, opening their arms in a hug. She is greeted warmly in the afterlife.

Page 26: Nefertari and Hathor, Goddess of the West (afterlife)
Page 27 and bottom of page 28: Hathor honored by Nefertari

- IV -

Hathor

Khepri   Osiris & Atum   Nekhbet (above doorway)   Hathor and Ra-Horakhty

Below: Nefertari making an offering to Hathor

Hathor

(Hwt-her)

Hathor as a cow, Nefertari Temple at Abu Simbel (dedicated to Hathor).

One of the noteworthy aspects of the Ancient Egyptian gods and goddesses is how fluid and amorphous they are. As their presence continued throughout the centuries of Egyptian history, their roles and relationships to each other morphed and changed with what was happening in the power structures of the times.

Hathor was an important goddess throughout all 3,500 years of the Ancient Egyptian religion. She was there as the consort of Horus in the earliest dynasties and shared an equal status* with the Goddess Isis at the end. The Isis temple on the island of Philae in southern Egypt – the last temple that actively practiced the Egyptian religion – was closed in 537 AD by the Byzantine (Eastern Roman) Emperor Justinian I.

Hathor with cow's ears, Hatshepsut's Temple, Luxor.

The animal that represents Hathor is the cow. There is an older cow goddess named *Bat* at the top of the Narmer Palette (an artifact from the beginning of Egypt's recorded history). That goddess also has the face of a woman, cow's ears, and horns on her head. But Bat's horns are curved inward, and Hathor's are longer and curved outward. However, Bat was incorporated into Hathor at the beginning of the dynasties, so most people refer to those images as Hathor.

The queen as Hathor and the king as Horus, King Menkaure. Old Kingdom (pyramid age).

* People who do not look for the hieroglyphs to know the names of the goddesses do not know that the two goddesses on the pylons of the Philae Temple are Isis and Hathor. (they think they are both Isis). Their equal status in the end is also apparent in that there is a Hathor chapel at the Isis temple and an Isis chapel at the Hathor Temple at Dendera.

Hathor of the West.
Larger, page 39.

Anubis, Hathor, Osiris.
Larger, page 33.

Another goddess that got incorporated into Hathor was Amentet. Her name means "the west." In Ancient Egypt, "the west" is a way to refer to the afterlife. It is similar to the way people today might say that someone is "on the other side." As Amentet merged into Hathor, one of Hathor's titles became "The Goddess of the West." There are two hieroglyphs for *west* – one with just a feather, the other with a hawk, as seen in Hathor's crown at left.

Hathor was the primary goddess in the afterlife during the New Kingdom (when Nefertari lived). An example of this is that at the beginning of the New Kingdom, the female pharaoh Hatshepsut's mortuary temple at Deir El Bahari has chapels for Hathor and Anubis.

During the height of the pyramid age, the goddess Isis had not yet become known. She was first mentioned in Dynasty 5, as the pyramid age was declining. However, 1,000 years later, by the time the New Kingdom began, Isis was already an important deity. She is often represented wearing Hathor's cow-horns crown, and if a person cannot read the names of the goddesses, it can be impossible to distinguish between them merely by their appearance. Examples of that on the left are from Nefertari's tomb.

Later, Hathor was described as the nursemaid for Horus as part of the Osiris and Isis story. During the Greek (Ptolemaic) period, there were festivals that linked the Horus Temple at Edfu with the Hathor Temple at Dendera, so Hathor was again a consort of Horus. As was stated at the beginning of this chapter, the roles of the deities were quite fluid and changed a lot during the different time periods.

Page 31: Hathor and Nefertari   Page 32: Anubis
Page 33: Prominent Netherworld gods – Anubis, Hathor, Osiris

- V -
Anubis

34

Anubis
(Inpu)

Like Hathor, Anubis was an important funerary god during the New Kingdom. He was the "undertaker" who prepared the body of the deceased. There are many representations of Anubis hovering over the body, actively engaged in the embalming process. There is another deity that looks like Anubis, Wepwawet, who is a guide in the afterlife, the "Opener of the Ways." As with many of the deities, the two get mixed together. Research in 2015 has concluded that he is not as jackal, as was believed, but rather an Egyptian wolf. Some of his epithets are: "Who is in the Sacred Booth," (see at right), "Who is in the Place of Embalming," "Lord of the Necropolis" (necropolis = cemetery), and "Who is in His Mountain."

ABOVE: Nefertari and Anubis   *Page 35: Anubis as an animal, Anubis with animal head*

- VI -
Horus

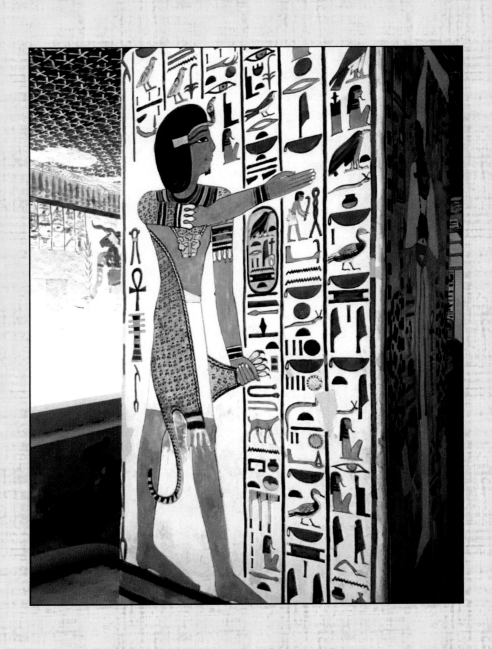

Son of Isis.

Horus

(Heru)

Throughout the history of Ancient Egypt, the king was considered "The Living Horus." One of the king's royal names was his Horus name. The animal associated with Horus was the falcon, a type of hawk. A number of countries today use symbols of similar birds. In the USA, it is the bald eagle.

The God Horus is represented in four different forms in Nefertari's tomb. They are as follows:

1. Ra-Horakhty, "Horus of the Two Horizons." This is a combination of Horus and Ra and represents the sun at it's height (noon). *See page 39 with Hathor.*

Horendotus, The Avenger of His Father.

2. Horus, "Son on Isis." *See pages 14 & 18.*

3. Iunmutef Priest, "The Pillar of His Mother" who protected her in her hour of need. Located on the left-hand pillar as one enters the burial chamber, he gestures to guide Nefertari at the beginning of her journey. He and Horendotes (#4) both wear the sidelock which indicates that they are young. The leopard skin garment shows they are priests. *See pages 36 & 37.*

4. Horendotes, "The Avenger of His Father." This refers to the story where Set, the jealous brother of Osiris, killed Osiris (the father of Horus in that story). It then falls to Horus to avenge his father's murder by killing his uncle. This idea of avenging the murder of a family member still occurs in the Middle East today. *Horendotes is pictured at left.*

*Page 36 & 37: Iunmutef Priest
Page 39: Hathor and Ra-Horakhty*

- VII -
Ra and Ma'at

Ra, The Sun

(Re)

Much of the Egyptian world view was intertwined with the sun. Ra *(Re)* is the primary solar deity. However, Ra gets combined with other gods, and the sun itself is part of the identity of other gods, as well. Khepri (pages 45, 48, 49) is the sun as it rises. Ra-Horakhty (page 39) is the sun at noon. Ra is usually represented with the head of a hawk but when he is the late-afternoon sun, he is a ram.

LEFT: The three stages of the sun's journey by day. *From the ceiling of the Tomb of Ramesses V & VI in the Kings Valley.*

BELOW LEFT: Nephthys and Isis are blessing Ra. See his hieroglyphic name to the right of the red solar disk. See also, page 41. The inscription to the right and left of his legs says that Osiris is Ra ("It is Osiris that sets as Ra") and Ra is Osiris. Ra's body is also in the mummiform of Osiris. Compare it to the image of Osiris on page 44.

When children first draw pictures of themselves, it is usually a circular shape. Arms and legs get added to this as their drawings become more detailed. So on a very basic level, the circle of the sun represents our primordial self. When the sun sets, it appears to travel under the ground through the night, so it traverses the "underworld" by night. The Egyptians envisioned the afterlife to be like that, too. Helpful information for navigating this journey was painted on the tomb walls. In these images, stories, and magical formulas, the person's identity is melded with the sun, and the sun's journey becomes their own.

Page 40: Ma'at   Page 41: Ra

Ma'at

Goddess of Truth and Justice

The image above has been reproduced thousands of times on papyruses for tourists and other paraphernalia. It emanates a sense of all being right in the world. Ma'at is the representation of choosing the good path, making the best choices, and doing the right thing even when we are tempted to do it differently. An easy way to understand her is that she represents the "rules of the game." If you play a sport, there are rules that need to be adhered to. Ma'at embodies those rules, but in this case, it is the rules of life, of a life well lived. Also spelled *Mayet*.

The full picture is on page 25.

Words spoken by...

daughter of Ra

Back on pages 4 and 18 of this book, you may remember the combination of glyphs for, "words spoken by" and "daughter of Ra."

The hieroglyphs can be read from right to left, left to right, or top down. On the top of this page, you will see that the ones above Ma'at's wings are read from right to left.

- VIII -

Osiris, Khepri, Akeru, and Bennu

See page 68.

Djed Pillar

Two ways to write "Forever"

Osiris
(Wsir)

Like many Ancient Egyptian deities, the role of the God Osiris morphed and changed throughout time. In the Old Kingdom (pyramid age), the god of the necropolis was Soker *(Seker)* but by the New Kingdom, that role was filled by Osiris. Osiris began as the god of farming, and in the legend* of Osiris and Isis, he was the good king who taught the people how to farm. He is shown with green skin (abundant plant growth) or black skin, the color of the rich Nile silt which created the fertile soil where the crops were planted. Also see on page 16 how he symbolizes rebirth.

One of the symbols associated with Osiris is the *djed pillar* which is referred to as "the backbone of Osiris." The hieroglyphic meaning is *stability*. The exact origin of the *djed* symbol is unclear. It is one of the earliest (pre-dynastic) symbols used, so is much older than the Osiris-Isis legend. However, it gets incorporated into the story as the Osiris pillar that Isis finds in Byblos.

Osiris was also called "The Lord of Time." There are two ways to write *forever* in hieroglyphs. When they are written one after the other, it is like saying, "forever and ever." You can see that written on the top in the middle near his crown on page 47.

In his hands he holds the shepherd's crook and flail. The shepherd's crook is the hieroglyph for *ruler*, so as king, he is "the good shepherd." The flail is a hieroglyph that denotes royalty. Osiris is the king of the underworld and sits on the judgment throne. So he is the one who "judges the dead." It is interesting to see how these same concepts get carried forward into Christianity more than a thousand years later. See: John 10:11, 10:14, Acts 10:42, 2 Timothy 4:1 and First Epistle of Peter.

Note: There are a number of versions of the Osiris-Isis legend. A quick internet search will find them, so they will not be retold and compared in this book.

Page 44: Osiris   Page 45: Khepri   Page 47: Osiris

Khepri

The Ancient Egyptian gods and goddesses were associated with different animals. The qualities these animals exhibit in the natural world were related to the qualities of that particular deity. Khepri is the scarab beetle. This beetle rolls dung into a ball that the scarab then pushes ahead of itself as it moves through the day. At night the dung-ball is buried in the ground.

This act was used as a symbol for the sun going underground at night and emerging in the morning, in a sense, being reborn each day. So Khepri, as the scarab beetle, symbolized rebirth and regeneration. Scarab amulets were also used as a protection symbol.

The illustration on page 42 shows the scarab as the sun in the morning.

Akeru (lions), Bennu (heron)
More of this wall on page 54.

Bennu The Bennu bird was also linked with both the sun and rebirth. Bennu is the *Ba of Ra*, (see page 24 for the *Ba*). One of the creation myths is that the world began as primordial waters out of which rose the land and the ben-ben stone. Bennu landed on top of it and called creation into being. Some Greek stories say that the Bennu bird periodically died and rose again, so was the predecessor of the phoenix bird.

Akeru Behind the Bennu bird is one of the *Akeru*, "the lions of yesterday (*Duaj*) and tomorrow (*Sefer*)." Part of the illustration on the wall of the tomb has been lost, but we know what would have been there. The *Akeru* are two lions that sit back to back with the sun and two-hills horizon sign between them.

Page 49: Khepri   Page 50: Ptah   Page 51: Thoth

- IX -
Ptah, Thoth, and Atum

See page 70.

Thoth (Djehuti)

The moon god, Thoth, is the god of wisdom and writing, and is the "patron saint" of scribes. Thoth can be both a baboon or an ibis bird. There are many statues of seated scribes with a baboon (as Thoth) perched behind their heads assisting them. The Greeks combined him with Hermes. In the New Kingdom, Thoth was the "Lord of the Eight," the **Ogdoad**. See that title next to him on page 51 – dish shape with eight lines underneath it. The Ogdoad were four pairs (male/female) of forces – water, eternity, darkness, and air. The Ogdoad cult center was near Amarna.

Atum

The solar god, Atum was the creator god of "The Great Ennead." This is the Egyptian creation story most well known today. Atum creates Shu and Tefnut, who in turn give birth to Geb and Nut. Geb and Nut have four children – Osiris, Isis, Nephthys, and Set. Atum is also represented as the sun at the end of the day.

See page 69.

The GREAT ENNEAD
Atum
Shu (dry air) - Tefnut (moisture/wet air)
Geb (earth) - Nut (sky)
Osiris - Isis - Nephthys - Set

Ptah

Whereas Thoth was the "patron saint" of scribes, Ptah was that for the artisans – those talented people who created all the beauty in Nefertari's tomb. The tomb workers lived near the tombs on the West Bank in the *Valley of Truth*. The name comes from one of Ptah's titles, *The Lord of Truth*. Both seated and standing, he is represented standing on a hieroglyph for truth, thus showing that he possesses it. Ptah is also a creator god, but the hieroglyphs tell us that, "He created the world with his heart and tongue." In other words, it was there in his heart, and when he expressed it, it came into being. This is the way of the artist.

See page 50.

Page 53: Atum

Bennu   *Nephthys as a kite (bird)*   *Osiris*   *Isis as a kite*   *Heh (million)*

Nephthys   *Re*   *Isis*

- X -
The Two Sisters: Isis and Nephthys

56

Look above the hieroglyphic name of each goddess to see where her name is on the wall.

Isis

Nephthys

Isis and Nephthys, The Two Sisters

Isis and her sister, Nephthys, were two of the children of Geb and Nut in the Ennead creation story. Unlike older deities such as Ra, Horus, Hathor, and Ptah, Isis was only first mentioned in the 5th Dynasty (pyramid age was declining).

However, her influence has been longer lasting than any of the others because there are still active Isis cults today. The Isis Temple at Philae, near the southern border of Egypt, was located near the trading center of Elephantine Island. The Nile cataracts made the river impassable for trading boats from southern Africa to continue north to the Mediterranean. The mixing of the trader's nationalities created a more diverse cultural atmosphere which enabled multiple faiths to be practiced there, thus allowing the Isis Temple to continue functioning after the other Egyptian religion temples were closed. See more about Philae, page 29.

Queen Nefertari and Isis

With the God Horus representing the king and Isis being his mother in the Osiris-Isis legend, Isis was often depicted with the king on her lap. She personifies the ultra-feminine characteristics of beauty and tender-heartedness. She is shown weeping for her husband after he is killed, tirelessly searching for him, and ultimately being able to heal him through love and her skills in magic.

Throughout it all, her sister Nephthys is there to assist her. Both Isis and Nephthys can be pictured as kites, a hawk-like bird of prey. See page 54.

Isis also overlaps with the goddess Hathor with representations of the two being virtually identical. Isis often wears the cows-horns crown of Hathor as pictured above. This is where knowing how to read their hieroglyphic names is helpful!

- XI -
Neith and Selket

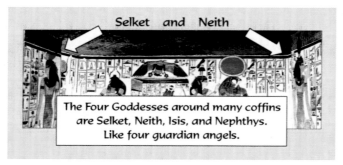

Selket and Neith

The Four Goddesses around many coffins are Selket, Neith, Isis, and Nephthys. Like four guardian angels.

In addition to guarding the coffins and sarcophagi, the four goddesses guarded the four canopic jars with the inner organs (as seen below for King Tutankhamen).

Neith guarded the east side and protected Duamutef, the jackal-headed god whose jar contained the stomach. The symbol on her head is a tool for weaving. Both **Neith and Selket** were known from the earliest records of Egyptian history and had many roles during different time periods. Neith was particularly associated with helping and protecting children.

Selket (Serket) guarded the western side and protected Qebehesenuef, the falcon-headed god whose jar contained the intestines. The symbol on her head is a scorpion. She was called on to protect people from poison and venomous stings and was associated with healing.

Above: Nephthys, Neith, Selket, Isis. Cairo Egyptian Museum, King Tutankhamen exhibit.

Page 58: Neith. Inset reads, "Words spoken by the Goddess Neith."
Page 59: At the top of the stairs, Neith is on the left and Selket is on the right.

Page 61: Selket. Inset reads, "Words spoken by the Goddess Serket."

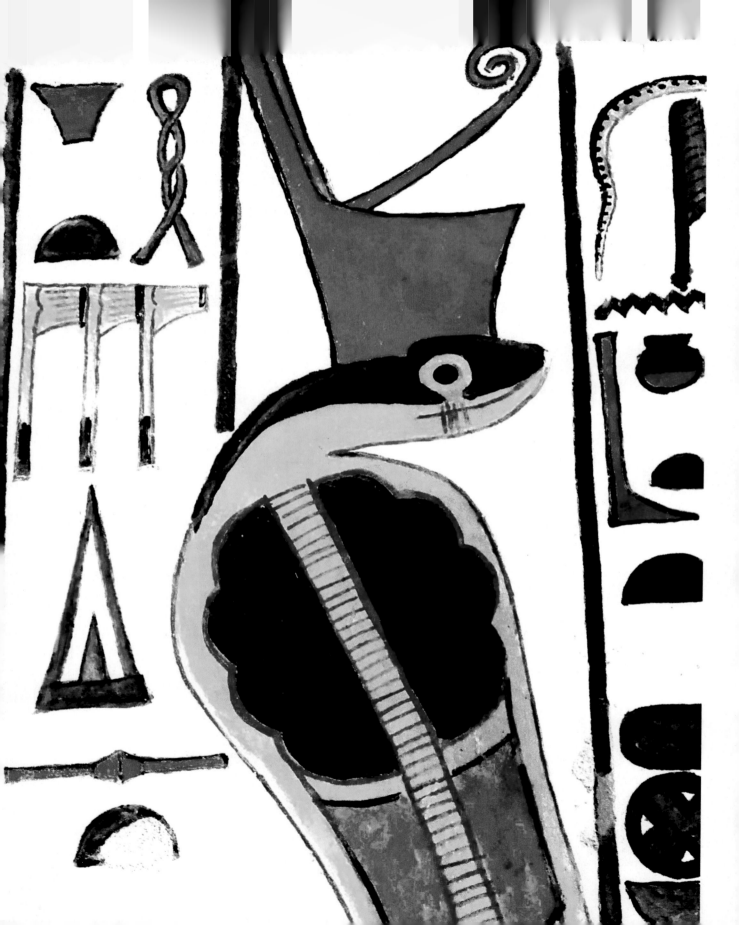

- XII -
The Two Ladies:
Nekhbet and Wadjet

Nekhbet, Goddess of Upper Egypt, "The White One"

Wadjet - Nekhbet
(or Uadjet, Udjo)
Lower - Upper
North - South

Their names are
written in hieroglyphs
to the left of
each of their crowns.

*Page 62: Wadjet (red crown)
but the hieroglyphic name
identifies her as Nekhbet*

*Page 63: The Two Ladies
surround Nefertari's
cartouche*

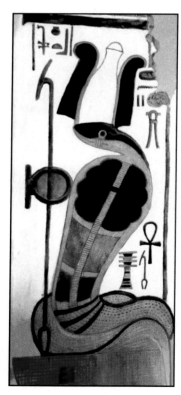

Wadjet & Nekhbet
"The Two Ladies"

Having things in duality achieved the balance that was of paramount importance in Ancient Egypt. Egypt was called "The Two Lands." In the south there were the floodplains of the Nile that created a fertile strip of habitable land within "the great sand sea" of the Sahara Desert. As the river approached the low lands bordering the Mediterranean Sea, it opened out into the Nile Delta area with multiple distributaries that created a wide expanse of greenery.

The **red crown** was for **Lower Egypt** (delta) and the **white crown** for **Upper Egypt** (higher land in the south). The Two Ladies were the goddesses who possessed these crowns. It was they who crowned the king, thus giving him the power to rule. **Wadjet** was the cobra of the northern delta and was called "The Green One." Her counterpart was the vulture, **Nekhbet**, "The White One" of Upper Egypt. Nekhbet could also be represented as a cobra, as seen on pages 63 and 64. On page 64 you can see her name written at the top – on the right going right to left and on the left side from left to right (look at the foot glyph).

Both of the Two Ladies are represented as possessing eternity (holding something in the hand/claw means to possess it). The symbol is in the vulture's claws and as cobras they are sometimes wrapped through it (page 63) and/or have it in front of them (see at left).

Eternity

Vulture Headdress

You may have noticed that Nefertari in often shown wearing a vulture headdress. This vulture is Nekhbet, but because the Goddess Mut is also  a vulture, there is an overlap with that symbolism, too. The vulture hieroglyph means *mother*. Hathor also wears the vulture headdress in one of the wall paintings and pairs it with cobra earrings (so, both of the Two Ladies).

Nefertari Tomb, QV 66, Valley of the Queens, West Bank of Luxor, Egypt

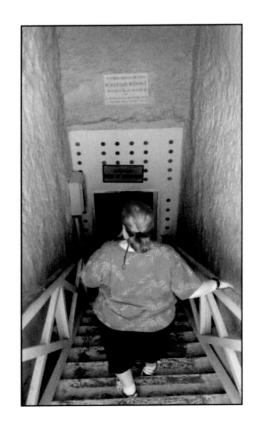

- XIII -
The Nefertari
Tomb Today

Nefertari presenting to the God Osiris

First discovered by Ernesto Shiaparelli in 1904, the tomb of Nefertari is breathtakingly beautiful. Those of us who have had the privilege to visit this tomb will remember the impact of viewing it until we ourselves enter the afterlife. Unfortunately, in the years after its discovery, the walls suffered considerable damage from moisture.

Beginning in 1986, the tomb was exquisitely conserved through a team effort of the Getty Foundation and the Egyptian Supreme Counsel of Antiquities. The walls were stabilized and the paintings were cleaned (no additional paint was added). *Note that some of the photos in this book have been partially altered.*

Nefertari presenting to the God Atum

The work took more than six years, but in the following decades, it has been a precious gift to everyone who has been able to witness its beauty.

Since the conservation was completed the tomb has fluctuated between being open to the public for short 10-minute visits and being completely closed when the moisture levels (from human breath) have reached unsafe levels.

Above: humidity sensor

Right above: ventilation hose

70 *Nefertari with Thoth*

One of the exciting things about this tomb is seeing all the hieroglyphs in color. The coloring of each glyph is not random, there is a specific color of each one. However, certain colors – like red and yellow – can be interchanged.

Above: stars on the ceiling of the first chamber

One lovely Ancient Egyptian idea is that after death, people become a star in the sky. Drawn like a string of paper dolls, it is easy to see them as our loved ones dancing happily as they look down on us.

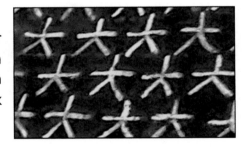

Constructing a tomb was a multifaceted and lengthy process. It makes sense that as the first parts of the tomb were dug out and made available, the artisans would begin their work of mapping out and later painting the walls.

In Nefertari's tomb the chambers on the higher levels have a bit of raised relief that gives the paintings a depth and vibrancy. However, in the lower burial chamber (which would have been completed later) the walls are mostly flat and the paintings have a different style.

The next two pages will give you a chance to compare the different styles.

Page 72: Nefertari with a guardian who looks like Taueret, the hippopotamus & crocodile goddess
Page 73: Nefertari

Horus   King Ramesses III   Set

Below: Back panel with the name of Ramesses III. Cairo Egyptian Museum

- XIV -

Missing Deities:
Sekhmet, Amun, Mut
Seshat, Nut and Set

Amun and Mut

Missing Deities

In the story of Osiris being cut into fourteen pieces, there is one piece which cannot be retrieved by Isis. And so with this 14th chapter, there are some gods and goddesses that were not included in Nefertari's tomb but still were prominent deities during that time. A few of those are included here.

Sekhmet, "The Powerful One"

Sekhmet was an important goddess throughout all of Ancient Egyptian history. She was the consort of Ptah, the god of Memphis (capital of Egypt during the pyramid age). See pages 50 and 52. There are more statues of the Goddess Sekhmet than any other goddess in Ancient Egypt. Her power was called upon when strength was needed, especially if people were sick with a fever. Her power and influence continue to inspire lovers of Egypt today.

When women attain positions of power, this can threaten those preferring a male-dominated system. This can be seen in the way that this powerful female deity was described in a story which was especially popular during Egypt's Greek era. Before the dams were built in southern Egypt (20th century), the Nile had cycles that included the annual flood that brought the rich Nile silt from the jungles of Africa to the river's floodplains downstream. It was this silt that created the fertile farmland, the Black Land of Egypt (*Kemet*). At one point in this cycle, there was a red algae that made it appear that the Nile water turned red. This red water was made into a delicious beer.

A story was created that this red beer was the blood of wayward humans who angered the gods. Sekhmet drank their red blood and became drunk. With her power sublimated, she transformed into the docile cat Goddess Bastet. How many men have desired to see a powerful woman lose her strength by drinking too much alcohol and becoming compliant? It isn't hard to imagine how this story came into being.

An interesting note is that even today the Egyptians believe in the power of Sekhmet. I kept suggesting to the people who carve and sell the statuettes of the gods and goddesses for tourists that they should make good statues of Sekhmet. It would help their businesses a lot. I did not understand why they repeatedly declined to do this. They made figurines of the other deities... They finally admitted the reason they did not was that if Sekhmet made them prosperous, Allah would punish them. So, they believed she had that power.

Amun and Mut

Another omission is the God Amun (*Amoun, Imen, Amen*), the supreme god during Nefertari's lifetime, and his consort, the Goddess Mut. Nefertari's name includes, "Beloved of Mut," but there are no wall images of that goddess in her tomb. *Page 75 is a beautiful wall relief of Amun and Mut from the mortuary temple of Nefertari's husband, Ramesses II.*

The Sky Goddess, Nut

Many of the tombs on the West Bank of Luxor have representations of the sky goddess, Nut, on the ceilings. Nut is also on the "ceiling" (the underside of the top) of coffins and also on the lids of sarcophagi. There are representations of her body filled with stars, giving birth to the sun, and the journey of the sun through her body.

Part of the ceiling of the burial chamber of the tomb of Ramesses V & VI, Kings Valley

Everywhere in Nefertari's tomb there are stars on the ceiling. Most of the goddesses in her tomb have the epithet, "Mistress of Heaven," and there are many *pet* symbols (the hieroglyph for *sky, heaven*) over most of the paintings, but no paintings of Nut as a goddess.

Set

One of the Great Ennead (see page 52) was the God Set *(Seth)*. Set's primary role seems to be to represent **opposition**. Everything in the Ancient Egyptian world had balance. There was Lower Egypt and Upper Egypt – the delta and southern

Egypt. The Black Land and the Red Land – the black silt that was farmed and the red desert that surrounded that strip of fertility along the Nile river.

Osiris was the god of farming and was represented with green skin (growing plants) or black skin (Nile silt). Set was the god of the desert regions. His skin is red like the color of the desert sand. The word for the color red in Ancient Egyptian is *deshert*. The desert is harsh, difficult, uninviting, dangerous. The fertile farmland is abundant with good food and ease. There are representations of the God Set teaching the king in the art of archery and how to fight. How do we become strong? Just as an athlete develops muscles by lifting weights, interacting with opposition pushes us to develop our strength.

There is a story (with multiple versions) of Set becoming jealous of Osiris and killing him. In that story, Horus is the son of Osiris and is then called upon to avenge his father's death through a series of battles with his Uncle Set.
See page 74: Set and Horus giving their blessings to the king.

Seshat

A goddess who appears on the walls of temples throughout Egypt, but who is largely overlooked by people today is Seshat, the consort of Thoth and the goddess of numbers. She can be seen on the temple walls participating in the layout of the temples and in counting the years of a person's life. Whereas, Thoth was the "patron saint" of writing, Seshat is the mathematician.

People are often curious about what the shape is on her head. It looks to them like a marijuana plant. My personal opinion is that it is a hemp plant. The way the Ancient Egyptians did their measuring (Seshat's area of expertise) was with hemp ropes. The laying out of temples (we know this from the pictures on the temple walls) was similar to the way a drafting compass is used. A series of intersecting circles provides reliable measurements when marking out boundaries in the sand. *These photos of Seshat are from Karnak Temple.*

About the Author

As the owner and operator of the *All One World Egypt Tours* business, Ruth Shilling, M.M., has traveled to Egypt 50+ times over the last 25 years. Sharing her love of Ancient Egypt – especially the gods and goddesses – with her travelers has been an ever-evolving pleasure. For those who feel the Egyptian connection, she hopes that this book will feed their desire to know more and to step for a while into the world of Ancient Egypt through the power of the images in Nefertari's tomb.

Like many entrepreneurs, Ruth has had a many-faceted career. She began in classical musician playing in orchestras in both the USA and Europe, as well as teaching at the University of Connecticut. Ruth also has taught various healing modalities, as well as personal empowerment strategies and spiritual development at centers throughout the USA. See the many books she has authored below (continued on the next page). Through her publishing company, *All One World Books & Media,* she now also publishes books by other authors.

See all Ruth's activities: ruthshilling.com

More Egypt Books by Ruth Shilling

Pictures of Ancient Egyptian Gods & Goddesses: Ruth Shilling's Photos (edited) taken in Egypt of the Gods & Goddesses

Egyptian Gods & Goddesses Notebooks
with pages that look like papyrus! 16 Volumes.

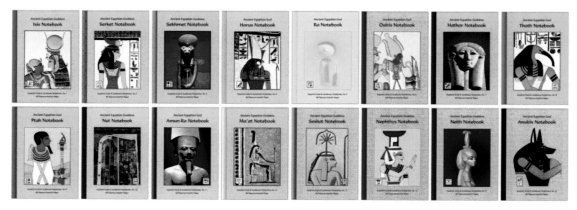

= More Books on the Next Page =

More Books and Cards by Ruth Shilling

ruthshilling.com

Time & Space in the Temples & Pyramids: All One World Egypt Tour

SINAI: The Desert & Bedouins of South Sinai's Central Regions (photos & text)

Accessing Clear Guidance: Help and Answers Through Inspired Writing and Inner Knowing

Clear & Free of Unwanted Thoughts & Emotions: 25 Effective Methods

Violin Success Series
• Success with the Violin & Life: Strategies, Techniques, and Tips for Learning Quickly and Doing Well, Volume 1
• Performing at Your Best: A Musician's Guide to Successful Performances, Volume 2

Through A Medium's Eyes Series: About Life, Love, Mediumship, and the Spirit World
• Rev. B. Anne Gehman, Volume 1 (also in LARGE PRINT)
• Carol Gasber, Volume 2
• Neal Rzepkowski, M.D., Volume 3

   The Color It True Manifestation Mandala Series, Volumes 1-4
• Marvelous Manifestation Mandalas, Volume 1
• Magnetic Manifestation Mandalas, Volume 2
• Miraculous Manifestation Mandalas, Volume 3
• Angelic Manifestation Mandalas, Volume 4

Ancient Egyptian Gods & Goddess Cards: godsgoddessescards.com

Facebook Pages

Egyptian Gods and Goddesses: facebook.com/EgyptGodsGoddesses
Ruth Shilling: facebook.com/ruthshillingmm
Egypt Tours: facebook.com/1worldtours